THE WEIGHT OF TRUTH

WHEN LIES BECOME THE ONLY REALITY

HOLLY HUNTER HARRIS

The Weight of Truth:
When Lies Become the Only Reality

A Journey Through Accountability, Deception, and Self-Reflection

The Weight of Truth:
When Lies Become the Only Reality

A Journey Through Accountability, Deception, and Self-Reflection

by
Holly Hunter Harris

Bell Street Publishing

Cover Illustration: Rodney Harris, Sr,

The Weight of Truth: When Lies Become the Only Reality

First Edition: 2024

Acknowledgment of Sources

The concept of the "shadow sell" was briefly mentioned, inspired by the work of Carl Jung. For readers interested in exploring this topic further, references to Jung's ideas can be found in works such as *The Archetypes and The Collective Unconscious* and *Modern Man in Search of a Soul.*

The weight of truth is heavy, but it is a weight worth carrying. It grounds us, anchors us, and sets us free. It reminds us that we are human—flawed but capable of growth, broken but capable of healing.
In the end, truth is not just something we owe to others—it is something we owe to ourselves.

— Holly Hunter Harris

Table of Contents

Chapter 1: Why Do We Ask "Why?"

"Why?" is not just a question—it's a spotlight, illuminating the gap between who we are and who we want to be. It lingers in the silence after a harsh word, the regret that settles after a wrong decision, and the unease we feel when we've crossed a moral boundary. Like a pebble in our shoe, it is a subtle discomfort we carry everywhere. The weight of "Why?" presses on our hearts, demanding an answer. Yet, more often than not, we sidestep it.

It's easy to ask this question of others. We demand explanations: "Why did you hurt me?" or "Why did you make that choice?" But when the same question is turned inward—"Why did I do that?"—the weight becomes unbearable. We want to avoid the possibility that the answer may reveal our shortcomings or insecurities.

At its core, the question "Why?" forces us to confront ourselves without the comforting shield of justifications. It demands honesty, which strips away layers of excuses we build to protect our ego. Admitting fault requires vulnerability—a quality that many associate with weakness. And yet, vulnerability holds the power to free us from the burden of guilt and the cycle of self-deception.

The Psychology of Avoidance: Why We Run from Ourselves

Avoidance offers a strange comfort. It allows us to pretend that what we did wasn't that bad, that someone else was at fault, or that our intentions somehow absolve us from the consequences. It tells us, "You're not a bad person; this was just a small mistake."

But avoidance isn't a solution—it's a delay. Unaddressed questions have a way of resurfacing at inconvenient times, catching us off guard. A casual conversation, a random memory, or a familiar face can trigger the guilt we thought we had buried. The more we run from the question, the heavier its weight becomes.

Psychologically, avoidance is a defense mechanism. Our minds try to protect us from pain, but this protection comes at a cost. Avoidance creates an emotional backlog—a reservoir of unresolved thoughts and emotions that seep into our everyday interactions. We snap at loved ones, withdraw from meaningful relationships, or sabotage opportunities because we carry unacknowledged guilt.

The Vulnerability of Accountability

Admitting that we have done something wrong requires us to stand emotionally naked without pretense or justification. It is an act of humility, acknowledging that we are not perfect and have failed ourselves or others. Accepting this is hard because it forces us to reckon with our flaws. We prefer the image of ourselves as capable, good-hearted, and competent—and mistakes disrupt that image.

Many people fear admitting fault will expose them to judgment or rejection, but accountability often brings connection. Vulnerability invites empathy. When we say, "I was wrong," we create space for others to say, "I've been there, too." Admitting mistakes doesn't make us weak; it makes us real. It strengthens our relationships, deepens trust, and fosters genuine growth.

The Burden of Unasked Questions
Some people live their entire lives without asking themselves, "Why?" They live on the surface of their emotions, drifting from one distraction to another, hoping to avoid the discomfort that self-reflection brings. But even if they never ask the question, the weight of their actions doesn't disappear—it follows them like a shadow, showing up in subtle ways. A person who refuses to ask "Why?" after hurting someone may find themselves increasingly isolated, their relationships strained by unresolved tension. A person who avoids asking "Why?" after a failure may never take steps to grow, remaining stuck in the same patterns.

The fear of asking "Why?" is often rooted in the belief that the answer will be too painful. "What if the truth about me is worse than I thought?" But the reality is this: avoidance is often more painful than the truth itself. When we ask "Why?" and face the answer head-on, we take the first step toward healing. The discomfort of honesty is temporary, but the peace that comes with self-awareness lasts.

The Stories We Tell Ourselves
We are all storytellers regarding our lives. We create narratives to make sense of our experiences, which are often riddled with bias. We cast ourselves as the protagonists, minimizing our flaws and emphasizing the weaknesses of others. "I only lashed out because they pushed me." "I didn't mean to hurt anyone." These stories protect us from shame but keep us from the truth.

The problem with these narratives is that they keep us stuck. When we blame others or minimize our actions, we rob ourselves of the opportunity to grow. Asking "Why?" disrupts these stories. It forces us to rewrite them with honesty and humility. While this process can be uncomfortable, it is also liberating. A story based on truth—however messy—will always be more meaningful than one built on lies.

Turning Toward Change
Many people live with the discomfort of unresolved

guilt because they believe that change is impossible. "What's done is done," they say, convinced there is no point in looking back. But the purpose of asking "Why?" isn't to dwell on the past —it's to learn from it. Every mistake carries a lesson, but we can only access that lesson if we are willing to confront what went wrong.

Growth requires reflection, and reflection begins with asking the right questions. "Why did I do that?" "What could I have done differently?" "How can I make things right?" These questions open the door to change. They allow us to turn guilt into action, regret into wisdom, and mistakes into stepping stones toward a better version of ourselves.

The Freedom of Self-Reflection
When we stop avoiding the question "Why?" and embrace the discomfort of self-reflection, we set ourselves free. We free ourselves from the need to maintain a perfect image, the burden of unresolved guilt, and the fear of facing our flaws. We become lighter, more open, and more connected to others.

Self-reflection is not a one-time event—it is a lifelong practice. It requires us to stay curious about our behavior, ask hard questions, and listen for honest answers. It is a practice of compassion, both toward ourselves and others. When we reflect with kindness, we recognize that being human means making mistakes. And when we own those mistakes, we create space for growth.

Closing Thoughts: The Power of Why
The question "Why?" is not meant to be a punishment but an invitation. It is an invitation to understand ourselves more deeply, to take responsibility for our actions, and to become the kind of people we aspire to be. It is a weight, yes—but it is a weight worth carrying.

When we stop running from the question and start asking it, we discover that the answers are not as terrifying as we feared. We find clarity, courage, and the strength to move forward. Ultimately, we realize we owe the question "Why?" to others and ourselves.

Chapter 2: Vanity and Its Mask

Vanity isn't just about outward appearances—it's about how we believe others perceive us and how we want to perceive ourselves. The invisible thread binds self-worth to image, making it fragile and dependent on external validation. Vanity is the voice inside us that says, "As long as they see me a certain way, I am worthy." This mindset doesn't leave much room for flaws, and when mistakes arise, the instinct is not to own them but to conceal them.

Admitting fault feels like cracking the mask we have carefully constructed over time. Beneath it lies the fear that, if others see our flaws, they will reject or judge us. For many, exposure is terrifying. Vulnerability in a world obsessed with appearances is seen not as a strength but a failure. The result? We keep the mask on, hoping no one will notice the cracks underneath. But the longer the mask stays in place, the more it isolates us from our authentic selves. We become prisoners of the very image we tried to cultivate.

The Social Mirror: Vanity and Perception

The modern world amplifies vanity through the constant presence of a "social mirror." Social media, professional achievements, physical appearance—everything is displayed, subject to judgment, comparison, and critique. Society rewards those who appear perfect. We see it everywhere: the flawless Instagram post, the airbrushed magazine cover, the humblebrag on LinkedIn. On the other hand, mistakes are met with shame or ridicule, leading people to hide their imperfections at all costs.

This pressure makes it difficult to admit fault. We begin to believe that admitting a mistake means diminishing our worth in the eyes of others.

Vanity creates a false equation:

Success = Worthiness, Mistakes = Worthlessness

We wear the mask of perfection not out of malice but out of fear. Fear that without it, we will no longer belong or be accepted.

The Danger of a Perfect Image
Fueled by vanity, perfectionism does more than prevent personal growth—it stifles authenticity—the obsession with appearing flawless leaves little room for authentic connection. Relationships become shallow as the need to uphold an image takes precedence over vulnerability. We start curating moments rather than experiencing them, performing rather than being.

Over time, the mask becomes a permanent fixture. People forget how to live without it, and self-awareness diminishes. When vanity becomes a shield, it blocks criticism and introspection. We begin to tell ourselves: "You didn't do anything wrong. Everything is fine. You are still the person you want to be." These lies provide temporary relief, but they also prevent growth.

The irony of vanity is that we weaken it to protect our self-worth. We distance ourselves from our true identity and fear being exposed. The mask offers safety but at the cost of authenticity.

Losing Ourselves in the Mask
When people rely on vanity to define their worth, they lose sight of who they are without the mask. They become the roles they play: the successful entrepreneur, the devoted parent, the social butterfly, and the intellectual. Each role is a persona carefully crafted to hide the parts of themselves they deem unacceptable. But over time, these personas erode the connection to the authentic self.

What happens when the mask cracks? When the carefully curated image no longer holds up under the pressure of life's challenges? For many, this moment of reckoning feels like a personal crisis. It is the point at which they realize that they have built their identity on external validation rather than inner truth.

The Trap of Vanity: Self-Deception
Vanity also fosters self-deception. When our sense of self-worth is tied to how others perceive us, we become skilled at justifying our actions. We tell ourselves:

- "I had no choice."
- "They made me do it."
- "At least I look like I've got everything under control."

These narratives are not just lies we tell others—they are lies we tell ourselves to avoid confronting uncomfortable truths. Admitting fault feels like dismantling the very foundation of who we are. Vanity whispers in our ear: "Don't show weakness. Don't admit you're wrong." But in reality, clinging to vanity prevents us from seeing the truth about ourselves.

Breaking the Cycle: Embracing Flaws and Imperfections

The first step toward dismantling the vanity mask is accepting that imperfection is part of being human. We are all flawed, and mistakes are inevitable. Admitting fault is not a sign of weakness—it is a sign of strength. It shows we are willing to learn, grow, and become better versions of ourselves.

When we embrace our flaws, we open the door to authentic connection. Vulnerability fosters trust, deepens relationships, and allows us to live more fully. We stop performing and start being. Once removed, the mask reveals a version of ourselves that is not perfect but real—and that is enough.

The Power of Self-Acceptance

Self-acceptance is the antidote to vanity. It allows us to see ourselves clearly without the distortion of external validation. It says: "I am enough as I am, mistakes and all." When we accept ourselves, we no longer need to wear a mask. We can admit fault without fear of losing our worth because our worth no longer depends on appearances.

Self-acceptance also gives us the courage to face the consequences of our actions. When we no longer fear being judged, we can make amends, seek forgiveness, and move forward. Accountability becomes an act of self-love rather than self-punishment.

Freedom Beyond the Mask

Living without the mask of vanity is liberating. It allows us to experience life fully without needing to impress or perform. It frees us from the burden of perfection and permits us to be human. We become more open, more empathetic, and more resilient.

When we no longer fear our flaws, we discover they are not obstacles but opportunities for growth.

The freedom beyond vanity is the freedom to be ourselves. It is the freedom to live with integrity, knowing that our worth is not determined by how others see us but by how we see ourselves.

Closing Thoughts: Tearing Down the Mask

Vanity is a mask we wear to protect ourselves from judgment but isolates us from the truth. It tells us that admitting fault will diminish our worth, but in reality, it is through accountability that we find actual value. Saying, "I was wrong," does not tear us down—it builds us up.

When we remove the mask, we discover that we are more than the sum of our achievements or the image we project. We are flawed but worthy, imperfect but whole. And that is enough.

Ultimately, the only image that genuinely matters is the one we see in the mirror—not crafted for others but reflecting who we are. When we let go of vanity, we reclaim our authenticity. Authenticity brings the freedom to live fully, love deeply, and grow endlessly.

Chapter 3: The Guilt That Lurks Beneath

Guilt is a subtle but persistent companion, trailing us like a shadow we cannot escape. It clings to us, slipping into quiet moments when we least expect it — during a conversation with a loved one, a silent car ride, or the pause before sleep. Even when we try to suppress it, guilt stays, demanding to be felt. It reminds us that something within us is unresolved. No matter how far we run from it, guilt finds its way back, infiltrating the spaces we leave unattended.

The Invisible Weight of Guilt

Guilt is often misunderstood as a fleeting emotion immediately after a wrong decision or action. But guilt is more insidious. It lingers even when the event that triggered it is long past and shapes how we speak, act, and think, often without conscious awareness.

We may not realize it, but guilt influences our everyday choices. It causes us to be more guarded in our relationships, to hold back joy, or to become overly defensive when criticized. Unaddressed guilt takes up emotional space, making us restless, uneasy, and disconnected from ourselves and others.

Others may not see the weight of guilt, but to those who carry it, it is authentic. Guilt presses down on the heart, making joy feel fleeting and peace seem out of reach.

The Ways We Bury Guilt

Many people respond to guilt by trying to bury it. They distract themselves with work, social activities, entertainment, or even toxic habits. We believe guilt will eventually dissolve if we keep moving and stay busy. But guilt is not quickly silenced. It lingers beneath the surface, waiting for moments of stillness to resurface.

Some try to mask guilt by rationalizing their actions:

- "I didn't mean to hurt anyone."
- "They misunderstood me."
- "It wasn't that bad."

These justifications provide temporary relief but don't resolve the more profound discomfort. The guilt remains, slowly influencing behavior subtly—through avoidance, irritability, or an inability to fully relax. We may even find ourselves withdrawing from relationships or activities that remind us of what we've done, isolating ourselves to escape the feelings we cannot face.

How Guilt Changes Us

Guilt, when left unaddressed, can change who we are. It limits our ability to be fully present with others, making us hesitant to connect deeply. It can distort our self-perception, leading us to believe we are unworthy of happiness or forgiveness.

We become defensive, unable to tolerate even gentle criticism because it reminds us of the guilt we are trying to hide. A simple question—"Are you okay?"—can trigger an emotional response disproportionate to the situation, not because the question is intrusive but because it threatens to expose the feelings we've been avoiding.

In this way, guilt doesn't just affect the past—it shapes the future. It limits our potential, preventing us from embracing new opportunities or repairing relationships. It becomes a prison we carry with us, restricting our emotional freedom.

The Prison Walls of Denial

Many people build walls to contain their guilt, hoping that if they seal it away, it will cease to affect them. They avoid specific topics, evade accountability, and distance themselves from situations that could expose their guilt. But these walls are not protective—they are restrictive. They don't keep the guilt out; they keep it in.

Living with unaddressed guilt is like carrying a hidden wound. The wound festers, unseen but ever-present, affecting every aspect of life. Denial may provide temporary comfort, but it also ensures the wound is never healing. Over time, the emotional toll becomes too great, and we find ourselves trapped by the very walls we built to protect us.

Guilt as a Call to Growth

Though guilt is uncomfortable, it serves a purpose. It is a signal that something within us needs attention. Rather than seeing guilt as an enemy, we can see it as a call to action—a prompt to reflect, make amends, and grow.

When we confront guilt, we take the first step toward healing. We begin to dismantle the walls we built, brick by brick, facing the truths we tried to avoid. This process requires courage and self-compassion. It requires us to say, "Yes, I made a mistake. But I am not defined by my mistake."

Acknowledging guilt is not about self-punishment; it is about self-awareness. It is about recognizing where we went wrong, learning from the experience, and committing to improve. When addressed with honesty and care, guilt becomes a tool for personal growth.

Making Peace with Guilt

The path to peace begins with acceptance. We must accept that we are human and will make mistakes and that guilt is a natural part of being alive. But acceptance doesn't mean resignation—it means taking responsibility for our actions and making amends where possible. Making peace with guilt also involves forgiveness—for others and ourselves. It means recognizing that we are not perfect, are doing our best, and are worthy of compassion. Self-forgiveness allows us to let go of the shame that often accompanies guilt and move forward with a sense of freedom.

The Power of Accountability
One of the most powerful ways to confront guilt is through accountability. Admitting our mistakes to others, seeking forgiveness, and making amends are acts of courage. They break the cycle of avoidance and allow us to escape the prison of guilt.

Accountability doesn't erase the past; it transforms it. It turns mistakes into lessons and regrets into opportunities for growth. We regain control of our narrative when we take responsibility for our actions. We are no longer defined by what we do but by how we choose to respond.

Letting Go of Guilt
Letting our guilt go is not about forgetting the past—it's about releasing the emotional burden we've been carrying. It's about permitting ourselves to move forward without being weighed down by shame. This process takes time and patience, but it is possible.

Mindfulness can be a powerful tool for releasing guilt. We learn to observe guilt without judgment by staying present with our emotions. We acknowledge its presence, reflect on its message, and gently let it go. Journaling can also help us process guilt, giving us a safe space to explore our thoughts and feelings without fear of judgment.

Closing Thoughts: Guilt as a Gateway to Freedom
Guilt is not something to fear—it is something to understand. It asks us to pay attention, to reflect, and to grow. When we confront guilt with honesty and compassion, we transform it from a burden into a gateway to freedom.

We no longer have to carry the weight of unaddressed mistakes or fear being exposed. Instead, we become lighter, more accessible, and more connected to ourselves and others. In the end, guilt is not a prison —it is a path—a path that, when followed with courage, leads us to healing, growth, and peace.

Chapter 4: Lies We Tell Ourselves

We tend to think of lies as things we tell others to manipulate, protect, or avoid consequences. But the most dangerous and insidious lies are those we tell ourselves. These are not lies spoken aloud—they live quietly in our minds, distorting our understanding of who we are and how we show up in the world.

We lie to avoid guilt, shame, or regret. We tell ourselves we are the victim, that we had no other choice, and that we did our best under the circumstances. These lies cushion us from the sting of hard truths. But over time, they begin to do more harm than good. They shape the narrative of our lives, becoming so embedded that we mistake them for reality.

The Purpose of Self-Deception: Protection from Pain
The lies we tell ourselves often begin with good intentions. They are coping mechanisms that help us navigate painful emotions—grief, guilt, shame, fear, and regret. Our minds instinctively try to protect us from discomfort, offering straightforward explanations to justify actions or avoid responsibility. For example:

- "I didn't mean to hurt them—it wasn't really my fault."
- "They overreacted. I was only doing what I thought was right."
- "If things had been different, I would have acted differently."

These small lies provide temporary relief. They keep difficult emotions at bay, allowing us to function without being overwhelmed by self-doubt or remorse. In the short term, self-deception may even feel like survival. But over time, these lies erode our sense of self and reality.

Living in a Fractured Reality

The danger of self-deception lies in how it fractures our perception of reality. Each lie builds upon the previous one until the boundary between truth and illusion becomes blurred. We tell ourselves one story to explain away a mistake, only to find that we need another lie to support the first. Soon, we live in a reality where half-truths and distortions become the norm.

In this fractured reality, we become disconnected from our true selves. We may no longer recognize the difference between what we believe and what is true, creating confusion. We might sense that something is off—that our relationships feel strained or are stuck in unhealthy patterns—but we struggle to understand why. The lies we tell ourselves become blind spots, preventing us from seeing clearly.

Common Lies and Their Consequences
Self-deception manifests in many forms, some more subtle than others. Below are a few common lies people tell themselves, along with the consequences they bring:

1. "I'm the victim."

> This lie allows us to avoid responsibility, framing ourselves as powerless in situations where we have agency.

> Consequence: We remain stuck in cycles of blame and resentment, unable to grow or heal.

2. "I did the best I could."

> While this statement can sometimes be true, it's often used to avoid admitting where we could have done better.

> Consequence: We miss opportunities for growth and improvement, repeating the same mistakes.

3. "It wasn't that bad."

> This lie minimizes the impact of our actions, allowing us to avoid feelings of guilt or shame.
>
> Consequence: Relationships suffer as unresolved issues build over time, eroding trust.

4. "They made me do it."

> Shifting blame onto others helps us avoid uncomfortable accountability.
>
> Consequence: We give away our power to change by denying our role.

Each lie offers a brief escape from discomfort but ultimately keeps us trapped. By avoiding the truth, we forfeit the chance to learn, grow, and create better future outcomes.

The Emotional Toll of Self-Deception

Self-deception may provide temporary relief, but the long-term consequences are heavy. Living in a fractured reality creates inner conflict. Some of us know that our story isn't entirely true. This disconnect between what we say and what we know leads to anxiety, stress, and a persistent feeling that we are not at peace with ourselves.

Moreover, self-deception isolates us. When we lie to ourselves, we also distance ourselves from others. It becomes harder to open up and connect authentically when hiding behind a false narrative. Relationships built on half-truths and avoidance become fragile and quickly shattered by misunderstanding or mistrust.

Why We Cling to Self-Deception
If self-deception is so harmful, why do we hold onto it? The answer lies in fear. Truth can be painful—it forces us to confront our mistakes, acknowledge the harm we've caused, and make complex changes. The lies we tell ourselves to act as a buffer, sparing us from this discomfort.

There is also the fear of losing our sense of identity. For many, self-deception becomes a part of who they are. Admitting the truth would mean letting go of the stories they've told for years, which have become part of their identity. This fear keeps people clinging to their lies, even when those lies no longer serve them.

Confronting the Lies We Tell Ourselves
The process of confronting self-deception is not easy, but it is necessary for growth. It begins with a

willingness to look honestly at ourselves and question our constructed narratives. This requires humility—saying, "Maybe I wasn't as right as I thought. Maybe there's more to this story."

Journaling can be a helpful tool in this process. Writing down our thoughts allows us to see patterns and identify where self-deception might be at play. Therapy or conversations with trusted friends can also provide valuable insight, offering perspectives that challenge our internal narratives.

It's essential to approach this process with self-compassion. The goal is not to judge ourselves harshly but to understand why we told these lies in the first place. Self-deception is often rooted in fear, insecurity, or unmet needs. Acknowledging these underlying factors can help us begin to heal.

Reclaiming Clarity and Integrity
The reward for confronting self-deception is clarity. When we let go of the lies we've told ourselves, we see ourselves and our lives more clearly. This clarity brings a sense of freedom—it allows us to be more authentic, present, and at peace with who we are.

With clarity comes integrity. Living with integrity means aligning our actions with our values, even when uncomfortable. It means taking responsibility for our mistakes, making amends when necessary, and committing to personal growth. Integrity is not about being perfect—it's about being honest.

The Power of Truth

Truth may be uncomfortable, but it is also liberating. When we stop lying to ourselves, we reclaim our power. We are no longer bound by fear or avoidance — we can make choices that align with our true selves.

Our lies keep us small, but the truth allows us to expand. It opens the door to new possibilities, deeper connections, and genuine transformation.

Closing Thoughts: Living Honestly with Ourselves

The lies we tell ourselves are like chains—they keep us trapped in old patterns and prevent us from becoming who we are meant to be. But the key to freedom is always within reach. It lies in the decision to stop hiding from the truth and start living honestly.

Living honestly with ourselves is not always easy, but it is always worth it. It brings clarity, integrity, and peace. It allows us to embrace our imperfections, learn from our mistakes, and grow into our best selves. In the end, we owe the truth not just to others but also to ourselves.

Chapter 5: Truth as a Fantasy

Truth, for some, is a distant ideal—something noble, even admirable, but far from their lived reality. To live truthfully requires effort, courage, and discomfort, and for those who live in denial, these demands are too much to bear. Rather than confront the truth head-on, they choose an illusion: a carefully crafted world where their lies are not lies but alternate versions of reality. They say, "This is just my truth," as though truth can be bent and shaped to fit their desires.

But truth is not subjective. It exists independently of perception, waiting patiently for us to face it. The deeper we sink into denial, the more truth becomes something we fear—a threat to the illusions we've built, the lies we've told, and the identity we've created. In time, truth becomes less of a reality and more of a fantasy— something that sounds good in conversation but feels unattainable in practice.

The Illusion of "Personal Truth"

In modern culture, the phrase "my truth" has gained popularity to validate personal experiences and perspectives. While it can be empowering to own our narratives, this phrase is sometimes misused to justify harmful behavior or avoid accountability. When we equate subjective experience with objective truth, we fall into the trap of believing that truth is whatever we want it to be.

For example:

- "I didn't lie; I just told my side of the story."
- "I didn't hurt them—they just chose to be offended."
- "This is my truth; no one can tell me otherwise."

These statements are not expressions of truth but attempts to avoid it. They blur the line between reality and perception, allowing people to live comfortably in denial. But the comfort they offer is temporary. Eventually, the truth—objective, unwavering, and unavoidable—comes knocking.

Denial as a Fortress Against Truth
is like a fortress built to protect us from the pain of truth. It keeps uncomfortable realities at a distance, allowing us to maintain the stories we've told ourselves. But the longer we live in denial, the more fragile that fortress becomes. Every new lie requires reinforcement; every avoided conversation adds

another layer of complexity, and every ignored fact brings us closer to collapse.

Living in denial means constantly managing the gap between reality and illusion. It's a delicate balancing act that requires emotional energy to sustain. This is why people trapped in denial often feel exhausted—they carry the burden of a false reality. They fear the truth will flood and drown them if they release their guard even for a moment.

Truth as a Threat

For those who have built their lives on illusions, truth is inconvenient and terrifying. It threatens to dismantle their identity, expose the lies they've told, and shatter the relationships they've built on pretenses. To face the truth would mean admitting, "I was wrong. I lied. I hurt people."

This level of honesty requires difficult humility. It demands a willingness to let go of the illusions that have provided comfort and control. It requires embracing uncertainty and accepting the consequences of past actions. Many people feel overwhelmed by these demands, so they continue living in fantasy.

The Emotional Toll of Avoiding Truth

Avoiding truth comes at a cost. It creates emotional tension as people are forced to maintain a version of reality that doesn't align with the facts. This tension shows up in various ways—chronic anxiety, irritability, restlessness, and a pervasive sense of unease. Relationships become strained, as the disconnect between truth and illusion makes genuine connection difficult. Trust erodes, both with others and with oneself.

The longer we live in denial, the more alienated we become from our authentic selves. We start to question our motives, intentions, and emotions. We become trapped in a cycle of self-doubt, unsure of what is real and what is not. In this state, the truth feels less like a possibility and more like a distant dream—something we long for but believe we can never achieve.

The Paradox of Truth: Liberating Yet Painful
The paradox of truth is that while it is liberating, it is also painful. It forces us to confront uncomfortable realities and take responsibility for the harm we've caused. But it also offers freedom—a release from the emotional burden of maintaining illusions.

Truth strips away the lies and defenses we've built, leaving us exposed and accessible. It brings clarity, allowing us to see things as they are, not as we wish them to be. And with clarity comes the opportunity for growth, healing, and transformation.

The process of embracing truth is not easy, but it is necessary. It requires us to sit with discomfort, face the consequences of our actions, and let go of the need to control how others see us. But in doing so, we discover that truth is not a fantasy —it is the foundation upon which a meaningful life is built.

The Path to Truth: Breaking Free from Illusion
How do we begin to break free from the illusions we've created? The first step is acknowledgment. We must admit to ourselves that we have been in denial and that our stories are not the whole truth. This requires humility and courage to say, "I was wrong."

The next step is self-reflection. We must examine the areas of our lives where we've been avoiding truth and ask ourselves why. What are we afraid of? What do we gain by holding onto these illusions, and what would happen if we let them go?
Finally, we must take action. Living truthfully means aligning our words and actions with reality, even when uncomfortable. It means having honest conversations, making amends, and committing to personal growth. It also means accepting that we are not perfect and that truth is not about being flawless but honest.

Truth as a Journey, Not a Destination
Living truthfully is not a one-time decision but a lifelong journey. There will be moments when we

slip back into denial and tell ourselves comforting lies to avoid discomfort. But each time we choose truth over illusion, we grow stronger. We become more resilient, authentic, and connected to ourselves and others.

Truth is not a fantasy—it is a practice. We cultivate it daily through small acts of honesty, humility, and accountability. It is a commitment to living with integrity, even when complicated. With each step we take toward truth, we move closer to freedom.

Closing Thoughts: Embracing the Reality of Truth
Truth may seem unattainable when we are trapped in denial, but it is always within reach. It waits patiently for us to stop running, to stop hiding, and to open our hearts to reality. When we embrace the truth, we discover it is not as terrifying as we imagined.

Truth does not destroy us—it sets us free. It allows us to release the weight of illusion, to live authentically, and to connect deeply with others. It reminds us that we are human—imperfect but worthy, flawed but capable of growth.

In the end, truth is not just something we seek—it is something we become. When we live with truth in our hearts, we transform our lives from fragile fantasies into solid, meaningful realities.

Chapter 6: Consequences of Avoiding Accountability

Mistakes are inevitable in life, but accountability transforms them from obstacles into opportunities for growth. When people refuse to admit their wrongdoings, the consequences are not just personal —they ripple outward, affecting relationships, institutions, and entire communities. Accountability acts as the bridge between error and resolution. Without it, unresolved mistakes accumulate like cracks in a foundation, weakening everything built upon them.

Refusal to accept responsibility creates cycles of avoidance, where people repeat their mistakes and grow increasingly disconnected from others and their potential. Accountability is not just about saying, "I'm sorry." It is about acknowledging harm, learning from it, and taking steps toward making things right when this essential act is missing, stagnation, broken trust, and missed opportunities for growth result.

The Personal Toll of Avoiding Accountability
Avoiding accountability creates an emotional burden that weighs heavily on the individual. People who refuse to take responsibility for their actions often find themselves trapped in defensive behavior, constantly trying to justify their choices or shift

blame onto others. This defense mechanism may protect their ego in the short term but creates internal tension. Over time, they feel more anxious, resentful, and disconnected from their true selves.

Moreover, avoiding accountability stunts personal growth. Each mistake holds valuable lessons, but when people refuse to face them, they miss the opportunity to improve. Instead, they become stuck in familiar patterns, repeating the same mistakes and experiencing the same frustrations. Progress becomes impossible without the willingness to reflect, admit fault, and change.

The Impact on Relationships: Eroding Trust and Connection

At the heart of every healthy relationship is trust. Trust is built on honesty, vulnerability, and the ability to admit when we are wrong. When accountability is absent, trust erodes. Apologies go unspoken, grievances pile up, and resentments fester.

Over time, the lack of accountability creates emotional distance between people. Partners grow frustrated, friends become distant, and family members stop communicating openly. When left unresolved, minor conflicts snowball into more significant issues threatening the relationship. Even when the original mistake is forgotten, the damage caused by the lack of accountability lingers, creating a divide that is difficult to bridge.

In romantic relationships, avoiding accountability can cause deep emotional wounds. A partner who refuses to admit mistakes forces the other person to carry the emotional weight of unresolved conflicts. This imbalance leads to frustration, insecurity, and, eventually, emotional withdrawal. Friendships, too, crumble under the weight of unacknowledged mistakes. Apologies left unspoken create lingering tension, and over time, friends drift apart.

The Psychological Trap of Avoidance
Avoiding accountability creates a psychological trap that becomes harder to escape over time. Each time a person deflects blame or denies responsibility, they reinforce the belief that admitting fault is dangerous and will lead to rejection, shame, or loss of control. This belief becomes a mental barrier, making future admissions of fault even more difficult.

Over time, the emotional toll of avoidance accumulates. People become hypervigilant, always on guard to protect their version of events. They may avoid certain people, conversations, or situations that remind them of unresolved conflicts. In doing so, they isolate themselves emotionally, cutting off opportunities for connection and growth. This isolation leads to frustration, bitterness, and a sense of being stuck—unable to move forward but unwilling to look back.

The Social Consequences of a Lack of Accountability

When accountability is missing on a larger scale, the consequences extend beyond personal relationships. Communities, workplaces, and institutions begin to suffer. Leaders who refuse to take responsibility for their mistakes erode trust among those they serve. When politicians, business leaders, or community figures deny their errors or shift blame, they sow distrust, disillusionment, and division. People lose faith in the systems that are supposed to protect and serve them.

The absence of accountability in families creates deep emotional scars. Parents who refuse to acknowledge their role in conflicts with their children send the message that accountability is unnecessary. This erodes the child's trust, leading to strained relationships and unresolved emotional pain. Unspoken apologies create tension in friendships, making it difficult to maintain meaningful connections over time.

Institutions, too, fracture when accountability is absent—workplaces where leaders avoid accountability experience higher levels of burnout, low morale, and employee turnover. Refusing to take ownership of mistakes stifles innovation and collaboration, creating a toxic culture where people fear admitting errors. Over time, these environments become breeding grounds for resentment, disengagement, and dysfunction.

The Ripple Effect: Broken Communities and Systems

At the community level, the absence of accountability creates cycles of harm. Conflicts escalate, and divisions deepen when people are unwilling to take responsibility for their actions. Social cohesion depends on trust, but trust cannot exist without accountability. Communities become fractured when individuals, families, and leaders avoid admitting fault or making amends.

The absence of accountability can also perpetuate systemic issues. Institutions fail to acknowledge their mistakes and lose credibility and public trust. Communities grow cynical, believing that change is impossible. This breeds apathy, disengagement, and social unrest. Societally, accountability is essential for justice, equity, and progress. Without it, systems become stagnant, resistant to change, and prone to corruption.

Why Accountability Is Essential for Growth

Mistakes are a natural part of life. They are opportunities to learn, grow, and become better.

However, growth is only possible when people take ownership of their actions. Accountability is not about assigning blame—acknowledging harm, making amends, and committing to do better. It is an act of integrity that requires humility, courage, and self-awareness.

Accountability fosters personal growth by encouraging reflection and self-improvement. It strengthens relationships by rebuilding trust and creating space for open communication. It promotes justice, fairness, and transparency, building stronger communities. It also establishes healthier workplaces by fostering a culture of honesty and collaboration.

Breaking the Cycle of Avoidance
Breaking free from the cycle of avoidance requires self-awareness and courage. It begins with small steps: acknowledging a mistake, sincerely apologizing, or owning up to a shortcoming. These small acts of accountability build momentum, making it easier to take responsibility in more significant situations.

It's important to remember that accountability is not a sign of weakness—it is a sign of strength. It shows that we are willing to learn from our mistakes, make amends, and grow. Accountability also sets an example for others, creating a ripple effect of honesty and integrity.

If you find yourself avoiding accountability, ask yourself:

- What am I afraid of?
- What story am I telling myself about what will happen if I admit fault?
- What would it feel like to let go of the need to be right?

These questions can help you move beyond fear and into a place of honesty and growth.

The Freedom Found in Accountability

There is freedom in accountability. When we admit our mistakes, we release ourselves from denial and avoidance. We no longer have to carry the weight of unresolved guilt or fear. Instead, we step into a space of clarity, honesty, and connection.

Accountability opens the door to healing. It allows us to make amends, rebuild trust, and move forward without the baggage of the past. It also deepens our relationships, creating space for authenticity and vulnerability. Most importantly, it allows us to grow

—personally, relationally, and spiritually.

Closing Thoughts: Owning Our Stories

Mistakes are inevitable, but accountability is a choice. When we refuse to take responsibility, we miss the opportunity to learn, grow, and connect. But when we embrace accountability, we reclaim our power. We show ourselves and others that we are willing to own our stories—flaws and all—and are committed to becoming the best versions of ourselves.

In the end, accountability is not just something we owe to others—it is something we owe to ourselves. It is the foundation of trust, the path to growth, and the key to living with integrity.

Chapter 7: Confronting the Shadow

The psychologist Carl Jung introduced the concept of the shadow self, a part of our psyche that holds everything we wish to hide—our flaws, fears, insecurities, unexpressed desires, and unacknowledged truths. We avoid confronting this side of ourselves because it doesn't align with the image we want to present. Yet, the more we deny the shadow, the more powerful it becomes. Jung believed that avoiding the shadow leads to inner conflict while integrating it leads to wholeness.

The shadow grows in the darkness of avoidance. It shows up unexpectedly—when we lash out at someone, repeat the same mistakes, or feel consumed by envy or shame. These moments are not random—glimpses of the shadow, calling us to pay attention. The more we suppress it, the more it controls us from the shadows. Actual growth only begins when we dare to confront these hidden parts of ourselves, bringing them into the light where they can be acknowledged, understood, and integrated.

What Lives in the Shadow?
The shadow contains the parts of ourselves that we reject or deny because we feel uncomfortable, shameful, or socially unacceptable.

These can include:

- Unresolved guilt from past mistakes.
- Insecurities regarding our abilities or worth.
- Jealousy and envy toward others.
- Fears of rejection, failure, or vulnerability. Unacknowledged desires that conflict with the roles we play in life.

- Anger is suppressed to avoid conflict or maintain appearances.

We bury these aspects of ourselves, pretending they don't exist. But just because we ignore them doesn't mean they disappear. They influence our thoughts, behaviors, and relationships, often in ways we don't recognize.

How the Shadow Controls Us
When we deny our shadow, it manifests subtly but destructively. We may project our insecurities onto others, criticizing them for traits we refuse to acknowledge in ourselves. We may become defensive, reacting with anger or avoidance when confronted with the truth. We might sabotage relationships or opportunities while wondering why things never work out.

The shadow also manifests in patterns—recurring conflicts, familiar mistakes, and feelings of frustration or helplessness. When we notice the same problems appearing repeatedly, it's a sign that the shadow is at work, trying to get our attention.

Avoiding the shadow drains our emotional energy. We spend effort hiding parts of ourselves, maintaining an illusion of control, and managing the consequences of unresolved issues. This leads to feelings of exhaustion, anxiety, and disconnection— from ourselves, others, and our sense of purpose.

The Courage to Face the Shadow
Confronting the shadow requires courage because it means facing parts of ourselves we would rather avoid. It involves admitting that we are not always the person we aspire to be—we have flaws, fears, and insecurities. But it is only by facing these truths that we can begin to heal.

Admitting wrongdoing is one of the most direct ways to confront the shadow. When we say, "I was wrong," or "I hurt someone," we acknowledge a truth we may have avoided. This act of accountability shines a light on the shadow, transforming it from hidden to acknowledged. While this process can feel uncomfortable, it is also profoundly liberating.

Shadow Integration: Becoming Whole
Jung emphasized that confronting the shadow is not about eliminating it—it's about integrating it. Integration means acknowledging that the shadow is part of who we are but does not define us. It's the process of bringing our hidden aspects into conscious awareness, accepting them, and learning how to express them healthily.

For example:

- When suppressed, anger becomes destructive, but when acknowledged, it can motivate us to set boundaries and advocate for ourselves.
- Insecurity can lead to jealousy, but it becomes an opportunity to develop self-compassion and confidence when understood.
- Guilt can weigh us down, but when confronted, it becomes a call to make amends and grow from the experience.
- Integration leads to wholeness. It allows us to accept ourselves as complex, imperfect beings. Our mistakes or fears do not define us, but we no longer need to hide them. We learn to live authentically, embracing both our light and our shadow.

Practical Steps for Shadow Work

Confronting and integrating the shadow—often called shadow work—is deeply personal and transformative. Below are some practical steps to begin engaging with the shadow:

1. Self-Reflection and Journaling
Start by asking yourself difficult questions:

- What am I avoiding in my life?

- Where do I feel defensive or reactive?
- Are there patterns or recurring conflicts I keep experiencing?

Journaling about these questions can help you explore your thoughts and emotions honestly, without judgment. Writing allows you to confront parts of yourself that might feel too overwhelming to address directly.

2. Notice Your Triggers

Pay attention to moments when you feel triggered—when someone's words or actions evoke a strong emotional response. These triggers often point to unresolved issues within the shadow. Instead of reacting immediately, pause and ask yourself: Why did this affect me so profoundly? What does it say about me?

3. Embrace Vulnerability

Vulnerability is essential for shadow work. It means being honest about your fears, insecurities, and mistakes. It also means sharing these truths with trusted people—friends, family, or therapists—who can offer support without judgment.

4. Practice Self-Compassion

. When confronting your shadow, it is essential to treat yourself with kindness. The goal is not to judge or criticize yourself but to understand and accept your whole self. Self-compassion allows you to embrace your flaws and mistakes as opportunities for growth.

5. Seek Professional Guidance

Shadow work can be challenging, especially when confronting deep-seated fears or past traumas. Working with a therapist or counselor can provide valuable support and guidance

.

The Freedom of Integration

When we confront the shadow and begin the integration process, we experience a sense of freedom. We no longer need to hide or pretend to be something we're not. We become more comfortable with our imperfections, more accepting of our humanity, and more connected to our true selves.

This freedom extends to our relationships as well. When we embrace our shadow, we become more empathetic toward others, recognizing that they, too, have hidden fears and flaws. We become more willing to forgive ourselves and others because we understand that imperfection is part of the human experience.

Living Authentically with the Shadow
Integrating the shadow allows us to live more authentically. We stop striving for an impossible ideal of perfection and instead embrace our whole selves—light and dark, strengths and weaknesses, successes and mistakes. This authenticity brings a sense of peace. We no longer need to wear masks or maintain illusions. We are free to be who we indeed are.

Living authentically also means being accountable. When we confront the shadow, we become more willing to admit our mistakes and make amends. We no longer fear the truth because we know that truth is the path to growth and healing.

Closing Thoughts: The Journey to Wholeness
Confronting the shadow is not easy, but it is one of the most important journeys we can take. It requires us to look inward, face uncomfortable truths, and accept the parts of ourselves we once tried to hide. But in doing so, we become whole. We stop running

from our fears and flaws and learn to live with integrity and authenticity.

The shadow will always be a part of us, but it no longer needs to control us. When we confront it with courage and compassion, we transform it from a source of fear into wisdom. And in that transformation, we find freedom to live fully, love deeply, and grow endlessly.

Chapter 8: The Liberation of Truth

Truth can be uncomfortable, even painful. It forces us to confront the reality of our mistakes, the harm we've caused, and the people we've hurt. Yet, as difficult as it may be, truth also offers liberation. There is a profound sense of freedom in owning our actions and taking responsibility for the consequences.

When we embrace truth, we shed the weight of guilt, denial, and avoidance that has burdened us. We stop running from the past and begin moving toward a future rooted in honesty and integrity. Admitting fault is not a sign of failure but a declaration of strength. It is the moment we choose growth over fear, integrity over illusion, and connection over isolation.

The Emotional Freedom of Truth

Carrying guilt or unresolved mistakes creates emotional tension. It forces us to live with a constant undercurrent of discomfort, even when we try to suppress it. No matter how difficult, owning the truth releases us from this tension. It is like opening the windows of a stuffy room, allowing fresh air to enter and stagnant air to escape.

When we admit the truth to ourselves and others, we experience relief. We no longer need to maintain a facade or keep track of lies. The truth simplifies life by aligning our inner world with our outer actions. There is peace in knowing that we have nothing to hide and nothing to fear.

The Courage to Say "I Was Wrong"

Admitting fault takes courage because it requires vulnerability. It means exposing ourselves to judgment, rejection, or criticism. It forces us to confront the fear that admitting a mistake makes us less worthy in the eyes of others. But in reality, the opposite is often true. When we say, "I was wrong. I hurt you. I'm sorry," we demonstrate strength of character. We show that we are willing to face discomfort for the sake of integrity.

Vulnerability builds connection. When we admit our mistakes honestly, we invite others to do the same. It creates a space for empathy and understanding, strengthening the bonds between people. It says, "I am human, and so are you. Let's learn and grow together."

Restoring Trust through Truth

Trust is fragile, and lies, avoidance, and broken promises easily damage it. When we fail to take responsibility for our actions, trust erodes. The people we care about begin questioning our motives, intentions, and ability to act with integrity.

But trust can be rebuilt through truth. Admitting fault and making amends is a decisive step toward restoring trust. It shows others that we are willing to take responsibility for our actions, even when it is difficult. It demonstrates that we value the relationship more than our ego.

Restoring trust takes time, patience, and consistency. It requires us to follow through on our promises and align our words with our actions. However, with each act of accountability, trust grows more substantial. The cracks left by past mistakes begin to heal, creating a foundation for deeper, more meaningful connections.

The Strength Found in Accountability

Owning up to our mistakes strengthens our sense of self. It aligns us with our values and allows us to learn from our experiences. Each time we admit a mistake, we become more resilient, self-aware, and capable of growth.

Accountability also empowers us to take control of our lives. We reclaim our honesty when we refuse to blame others or make excuses. We stop being victims of circumstance and actively participate in our growth. Mistakes are no longer obstacles—they become stepping stones toward personal development.

The Transformational Power of Apology
Apologizing is not just about saying, "I'm sorry." A sincere apology acknowledges the harm caused, takes responsibility, and expresses a genuine desire to make things right. It means saying, "I see the impact of my actions, and I care enough to change."

Apologies can heal both the person offering them and the person receiving them. For the person offering the apology, it brings closure and emotional release. For the person receiving it, it provides validation and opens the door to forgiveness.

The most transformative apologies are accompanied by action—efforts to make amends and prevent the mistake from happening again. These actions reinforce the sincerity of the apology and demonstrate a commitment to growth.

Becoming More Than Our Mistakes
Our mistakes do not define us but how we respond to them. Every time we admit a mistake and choose to make amends, we grow in character. We become more than the sum of our errors—we become people of integrity.

Character is built when we take ownership of our actions, learn from our failures, and strive to improve. It is forged in our choices when no one is watching and in the apologies we offer without expectation of reward. These moments of truth shape who we are and determine the quality of our relationships, both with others and with ourselves.

The Ripple Effect of Truth
The liberation from truth extends beyond the individual—it creates a ripple effect. When we embrace truth in our own lives, we inspire others to do the same. Our example becomes a light, encouraging those around us to live with honesty and integrity.

Truth fosters trust and connection in families, workplaces, and communities. It creates environments where people feel safe to be vulnerable and where mistakes are seen not as failures but as opportunities for growth. This ripple effect strengthens relationships, promotes healing, and builds more substantial, resilient communities.

Letting Go of Perfectionism
One of the barriers to truth is the fear of being seen as imperfect. Many people avoid admitting fault because they believe they must appear flawless to be worthy of love and respect. But the pursuit of perfection is a trap. It disconnects us from our humanity and isolates us from others.

We create space for truth when we let go of the need to be perfect. We recognize that making mistakes is part of being human and that admitting those mistakes is an act of courage, not weakness. We stop striving for an impossible ideal and embrace life's messy, imperfect reality.
Truth as a Path to Freedom
Truth is not always easy, but it is always worth it. It frees us from the burden of guilt, the tension of denial, and the fear of being exposed. It allows us to live authentically without the need for masks or excuses.

The freedom found in truth is the freedom to be fully ourselves—flawed, growing, and worthy. It is the freedom to connect deeply with others, knowing that we are accepted not for our perfection but for our authenticity. It is the freedom to move forward, unburdened by the weight of unresolved mistakes.

Closing Thoughts: The Power of Truth to Transform

Truth is liberating. It brings clarity, restores trust, and creates space for growth. It allows us to learn from our mistakes, make amends, and become people of character. Each time we choose truth over denial, we step into our power. We show the world—and ourselves—that we are willing to grow, change, and live with integrity.

In the end, truth is not just something we offer to others—it is a gift we give ourselves. It sets us free from the past, empowers us in the present, and opens the door to a future built on honesty and trust. The liberation of truth is not just the absence of lies—it is the presence of authenticity, courage, and connection.

Chapter 9: How to Take Ownership of Your Life

Accountability is more than just a concept—it is a practice, a way of being in the world. It is about showing up fully in your life, owning your actions, and taking responsibility for their impact on yourself and others. While it is easy to shift blame or make excuses, real growth begins when we take ownership of our mistakes and decisions.

Taking ownership of your life is not a one-time event but a habit that must be cultivated over time. It requires a willingness to confront uncomfortable truths, a commitment to self-improvement, and the humility to acknowledge when we fall short. But the rewards of accountability are immense: they bring clarity, strengthen relationships, and empower us to live with integrity and intention.

The Foundation of Accountability: Small, Intentional Steps

Taking ownership of your life doesn't happen immediately. It begins with small steps —moments when you act honestly and take responsibility for your actions. These steps may seem small, but they build momentum over time, creating a foundation for greater accountability.

1. Acknowledge Your Mistakes

- Start by recognizing when you've made a mistake, even if it feels uncomfortable.
- Avoid the temptation to blame others or make excuses. Instead, say to yourself: "I made this choice, and I need to take responsibility for it."

2. Apologize Sincerely

- If your actions have hurt someone, offer a genuine apology.
- A good apology acknowledges the harm caused, expresses regret, and is willing to make amends.
- Example: "I realize my words hurt you. I am sorry, and I want to make it right."

3. Make Amends Where Possible

- Taking responsibility means not just saying "sorry" but also taking action to repair the harm.
- Ask, "What can I do to improve this?" This shows that you are committed to real change.

Self-Reflection: The Key to Personal Growth
Self-reflection is essential to owning your life. It allows you to examine your actions, understand your motivations, and recognize patterns in your behavior. Without reflection, repeating mistakes or staying stuck in unhealthy patterns is easy.

Journaling:

Writing in a journal lets you explore your thoughts and emotions without judgment. It helps you process experiences, identify areas for growth, and gain clarity on your actions.

Journal Prompts for Accountability:

- What mistake did I make recently, and what can I learn?
- Is there anyone I need to apologize to?
- How did I handle a challenging situation? What would I do differently next time?

Reflection Questions to Build Awareness:

- Am I acting in alignment with my values?
- Where am I making excuses in my life?
- How can I take more responsibility for my actions and choices?

The Role of Therapy in Building Accountability

Sometimes, taking ownership of your life requires more profound emotional work. Therapy provides a supportive space to explore past experiences, work through difficult emotions, and develop healthier coping mechanisms. A therapist can guide you through the process of self-reflection and help you build the tools necessary to cultivate accountability.

Therapy is beneficial when:

- You struggle to understand why you avoid responsibility.

- Unresolved guilt or shame is holding you back.

- You want to break free from patterns of blame and defensiveness.

Seeking therapy is not a sign of weakness—it is a sign of strength. It shows a willingness to grow, learn, and take responsibility for one's emotional well-being.

The Practice of Mindfulness: Responding with Intention

Mindfulness is the practice of staying present in the moment without judgment. It helps you become more aware of your thoughts, emotions, and actions, allowing you to respond to situations with intention rather than react out of habit.

How Mindfulness Supports Accountability:

- It increases self-awareness, helping you recognize when you are avoiding responsibility.
- It allows you to pause before reacting, giving you the space to choose a more intentional response.
- It helps you stay grounded in the present moment, allowing you to address challenges

as they arise rather than avoiding them.

Simple Mindfulness Practices to Build Accountability:

1.1.Pause and Breathe: When you feel triggered or defensive, take a deep breath before responding.

1.2.
Body Scan: Check in with your body throughout the day. Notice where you feel tension or discomfort. These sensations can be signs that you are avoiding something.

1.3.Daily Reflection: At the end of each day, spend a few minutes reflecting on your actions. Ask yourself, "Did I take responsibility today? "If not, what held me back? "

Breaking the Habit of Blame and Excuses

Blame and excuses are defense mechanisms that protect us from discomfort but prevent us from growing. To take ownership of your life, you must become aware of these patterns and consciously choose to break them.

- How to Recognize When You Are Blaming or Making Excuses:

- Are you focusing on what others did wrong instead of your role?
  - Are you using phrases like, "If only they hadn't..." or "I couldn't help it because..."?

- **What to Do Instead:**

  - Shift your focus to what you can control: "What could I have done differently?"
  - Practice self-compassion: "It's okay to make mistakes. What matters is that I learn from them."

Breaking free from blame and excuses is not easy but essential for personal growth. It allows you to take full responsibility for your actions and empowers you to make meaningful changes in your life.

Aligning Your Actions with Your Values
Living with accountability means aligning your actions with your values. It requires you to act in ways that reflect what you care about most, even when difficult or inconvenient.

- **Identify Your Core Values:**

Take some time to reflect on what matters most to you.

Some examples of core values include:

> Honesty
> Compassion
> Integrity
> Responsibility
> Growth

Ask yourself:
Are my actions aligned with my values?

Where am I falling short, and how can I do better?

When your actions align with your values, you experience a sense of fulfillment and authenticity. You no longer need to hide behind excuses or avoid responsibility because you live in alignment with who you are.

The Power of Forgiveness in Accountability
Taking ownership of your life also involves forgiving yourself and others. Mistakes are inevitable, and holding onto guilt or resentment only creates emotional burdens. Forgiveness allows you to release these burdens and move forward with clarity.

- **Self-Forgiveness:**

   Acknowledge your mistakes, take responsibility, and commit to doing better. Then, let go of the guilt. Self-forgiveness is essential to growth—it frees you from the past and empowers you to create a better future.

- **Forgiving Others:**

   Holding onto resentment keeps you stuck in a cycle of blame. Forgiving others doesn't mean excusing their behavior—it means releasing your attachment to the hurt so that you can move forward.

The Freedom Found in Ownership
When you take ownership of your life, you experience a profound sense of freedom. Excuses, defensiveness, or blame no longer bind you. You become empowered to make choices that align with your values and create the life you want to live.

Ownership also brings peace of mind. You no longer have to carry the emotional weight of unresolved mistakes or unspoken apologies. You become more connected to yourself and others, building relationships based on trust and authenticity.

Closing Thoughts: Embracing the Responsibility of Growth

Taking ownership of your life is not about being perfect—it's about being accountable. It's about recognizing mistakes, learning from them, and striving to improve. It's about aligning your actions with your values and building a life of integrity, intention, and authenticity.

The journey toward accountability is not always easy but worth it. Each step brings you closer to the person you aspire to be. It strengthens your relationships, empowers you to grow, and allows you to live peacefully and purposefully.

Ultimately, ownership is not something you owe to others—it is a gift you give yourself. It is the key to personal freedom, growth, and fulfillment.

Chapter 10: Building a World Where Truth Prevails

Imagine a world where people embrace accountability not as a burden but as a gift—where admitting mistakes is celebrated as a sign of strength, not weakness. In this world, truth is valued in public discourse and private conversations, as well as in families, workplaces, and institutions. Mistakes would not be seen as failures but as stepping stones to wisdom.

In a world where truth prevails, people no longer need to hide behind excuses or facades. Vulnerability would be encouraged, creating space for connection, trust, and growth. Relationships would deepen because people would know that honesty does not mean losing love or respect—it means building it.

What would it take to create this world? The road to such a place is not paved with grand gestures but small, everyday actions. It begins with each of us choosing truth over convenience, humility over pride, and accountability over avoidance. Though the weight of truth may feel heavy, it is also freeing—it allows us to let go of the burdens of denial, guilt, and fear.

The Power of Honest Relationships
In a world where truth is honored, relationships thrive. People would feel safe admitting when they are wrong, knowing that mistakes are not the end of the road but the beginning of transformation. Conversations would become more meaningful, with less need for pretense or defensiveness. Partners would trust each other deeply, friends would grow closer, and families would heal from past hurts.

Honesty builds bridges between people. It creates a foundation of trust that allows relationships to weather challenges and conflicts. When people embrace accountability, they learn that conflict is not something to fear—it is an opportunity to understand each other better and grow together. The more we practice honesty in our relationships, the stronger and more resilient they become.

Communities Rooted in Truth and Accountability
A community built on truth is one where individuals feel empowered to act with integrity. Leaders take responsibility for their decisions, institutions admit their shortcomings, and members work together toward solutions. Trust between people and systems would be restored as accountability becomes the norm rather than the exception.

Such communities thrive because people know they are supported—not despite their flaws, but because of them. Mistakes are addressed openly, and solutions are created collaboratively. When truth prevails, communities become more robust, inclusive, and just. Imagine institutions that admit their mistakes, schools that teach students the value of accountability, and workplaces where employees feel safe admitting errors and learning from them. In these environments, innovation and collaboration flourish because a learning culture replaces the fear of failure.

The Transformative Impact of Personal Accountability

Creating a world where truth prevails begins on an individual level. Each of us has the power to create change through the choices we make every day. When we choose accountability, we lead by example, inspiring others to do the same. Our actions create a ripple effect, influencing the people around us and fostering a culture of honesty.

Imagine a world where children grow up watching their parents admit mistakes and take responsibility. These children would learn that truth is not something to fear but to embrace. They would grow into adults who know that mistakes are part of life and that accountability leads to growth. Generations would benefit from a culture where honesty is celebrated, trust is nurtured, and people are empowered to live authentically.

Choosing Truth Over Convenience

One of the most significant challenges of embracing truth is that it often feels inconvenient. It is easier to tell a white lie than admit fault and shift blame than to own a mistake. But these shortcuts only offer temporary relief, while truth creates lasting freedom. Building a world where truth prevails requires us to make conscious choices every day:

- Apologize when we are wrong, even when it feels uncomfortable.

- Admit mistakes without deflecting or making excuses.
- Speak honestly with loved ones, even when it feels risky.
- Hold ourselves accountable for our words and actions, knowing that accountability is the path to personal growth.

These small acts of honesty may seem insignificant, but they have a profound impact. Each time we choose truth, we become more aligned with our values. We build trust with others, strengthen our relationships, and grow as individuals. The world changes when enough people make these small, courageous daily choices.

The Road Ahead: A Lifelong Commitment to Truth

Creating a world where truth prevails is not a one-time effort but a lifelong journey. There will be moments when the weight of truth feels overwhelming and when the temptation to avoid responsibility is vital. But each time we choose truth, we strengthen our ability to carry its weight. We become more resilient, connected, and at peace with ourselves and others.

This journey requires patience and perseverance. Mistakes will still happen, and there will be times when we fall short. But what matters is not that we are perfect but committed to learning, growing, and living with integrity.

Closing Thoughts: Embracing the Weight of Truth
The weight of truth is heavy, but it is a weight worth carrying. It grounds us in reality, anchoring us to what matters most—our values, relationships, and sense of purpose. It reminds us that we are human—flawed but capable of growth, broken but capable of healing.

Truth allows us to live fully without guilt or the fear of being exposed. It will enable us to embrace our mistakes, make amends, and build relationships rooted in trust and authenticity. It empowers us to create meaningful change in our lives, communities, and the world.

In the end, truth is not just something we owe to others—it is something we owe to ourselves. It is the foundation of a well-lived life, where we can be who we are. When we carry the weight of truth with courage and grace, we discover that it is not a burden but a gift.
And so, the road to a better world begins with each of us. It starts with small acts of honesty, the courage to

admit we are wrong, and the commitment to live with integrity. Together, we can build a world where truth prevails—a world where mistakes are met with compassion, growth is celebrated, and people can live authentically.

This is the power of truth. This is the weight we carry. And this is the freedom we find when we choose to embrace it.

Bell Street Publishing

Other books you may enjoy reading from Bell Street Publishing:

About the Author

Holly Hunter Harris, a Canton, Ohio native, explores the complexities of truth, accountability, and self-awareness in 'The Weight of Truth: When Lies Become the Only Reality.'
With a deep passion for personal growth, Holly encourages readers to confront uncomfortable truths and embrace the power of self-reflection.
When not writing, Holly enjoys road trips, general aviation, editing novels, and still photography. She draws from life's experiences to inspire authentic writing. This book reflects the belief that honesty with oneself is not a burden but a path to healing, transformation, and freedom.